How Much Can a Bare Bear Bear?

What Are Homonyms and Homophones?

To my sister Mary,
who was merry on the day
she was to marry

—B.P.C.

Homonyms:
Two or more words that
are pronounced the same
and spelled the same but
have different meanings

Homophones:
Two or more words that
are pronounced the same
but have different spellings
and different meanings

How Much Can a Bare Bear Bear?

What Are Homonyms and Homophones?

by Brian P. Cleary

illustrated by Brian Gable

M MILLBROOK PRESS / MINNEAPOLIS

Homonyms

are words that sound
and also look alike.

But they have
different meanings, as in
"Can you pass that can, Mike?"

Or "May I sail with you in May and coast all along the coast?"

These words are a blast
if you say them quite fast.

like

"Why don't we toast with some toast?"

A light may be light,
like a small paper kite.

A trunk can be found
in a trunk.

An inchworm or snail could scale a scale.

A lean cat could lean on a skunk.

But punch cannot punch,
and at breakfast
or lunch,

your jam cannot jam
on a trumpet.

A bowl cannot bowl,
but a roll
might just roll
if it's not
made as flat
as a crumpet.

Now, some words sound identical but are spelled in different ways. These words are known as **homophones,**

like
praise

and preys

and prays.

Though **homophones** have matching sounds, **their** meanings aren't the same.

And there isn't any question,
they're as fun as any game.

A horse can get hoarse
from talking, of course.

A ewe
could take you
on a stroll.

A fowl can be foul.
A toad can be towed.
An heir mustn't err in the air.

A Whale can Wail.

A male can mail.
A pair might just
pare a big pear.

A bust can be bused
by a driver you trust,

and Barry
can bury
a berry.

A band could be banned
if they get out of hand,

and **Mary** (who's **merry**)
can **marry**.

But the sea cannot see,
and it's clear as can be
that a ball will not bawl when it's rolled.

A moose has no use
for a bottle of mousse,

and a creek doesn't creak
when it's old.

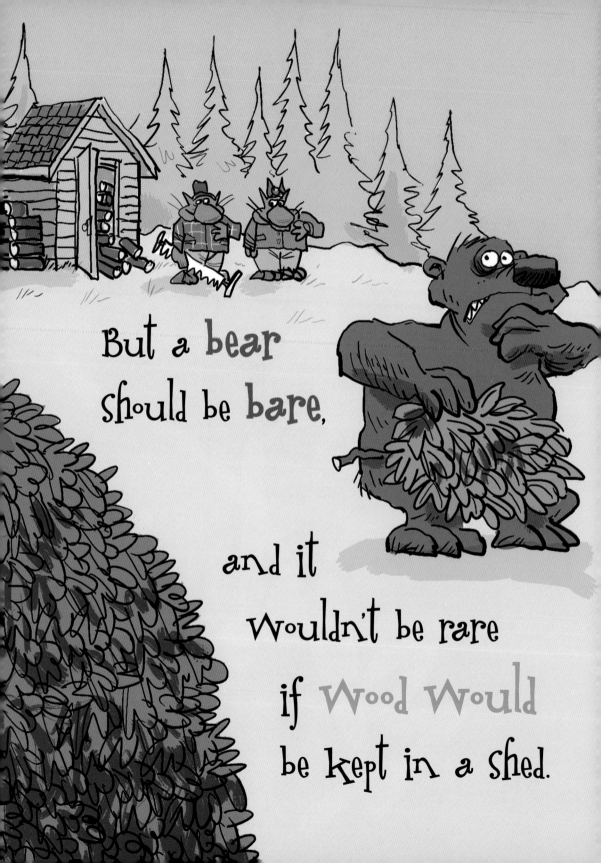

But a bear
should be bare,

and it
wouldn't be rare
if Wood Would
be kept in a shed.

A Sioux
might not Sue
if he knew
that the gnu that he bought
wasn't new like you said.

My niece could see Grease
both in Greece and in Nice.

A Czech could be
writing a
check.

A **maid** could be **made**
to be very afraid
When she **heard**
a big **herd** on the deck.

So, what are **homonyms** and **homophones**?

Do you know?

ABOUT THE AUTHOR & ILLUSTRATOR

BRIAN P. CLEARY is the author of the best-selling Words Are CATegorical® series as well as the Math Is CATegorical®, Food Is CATegorical™, Adventures in Memory™, and Sounds Like Reading® series. He has also written Six Sheep Sip Thick Shakes: And Other Tricky Tongue Twisters, The Punctuation Station, and several other books. Mr. Cleary lives in Cleveland, Ohio.

BRIAN GABLE is the illustrator of many Words Are CATegorical® books and the Math Is CATegorical® series. Mr. Gable also works as a political cartoonist for the Globe and Mail newspaper in Toronto, Canada.

Millbrook Press
A division of Lerner Publishing Group, Inc.
241 First Avenue North
Minneapolis, MN 55401 USA

For reading levels and more information, look up this title at www.lernerbooks.com.

Library of Congress Cataloging-in-Publication Data

Cleary, Brian P., 1959—
    How much can a bare bear bear? : what are homonyms and homophones? /
by Brian P. Cleary ; illustrated by Brian Gable.
    p.   cm. — (Words are categorical)
    ISBN 978—1—57505—824—5 (lib. bdg. : alk. paper)
    ISBN 978—0—8225—6362—4 (EB pdf)
    1. English language—Homonyms—Juvenile literature. I. Gable, Brian,1949—
ill. II. Title.
PE1595.C58 2005
428.1—dc22   2004031106

Manufactured in China
14-41677-5347-3/23/2016